ATE!

JOSEPH'S JOURNAL
THIS BOOK BELONGS TO:

Me

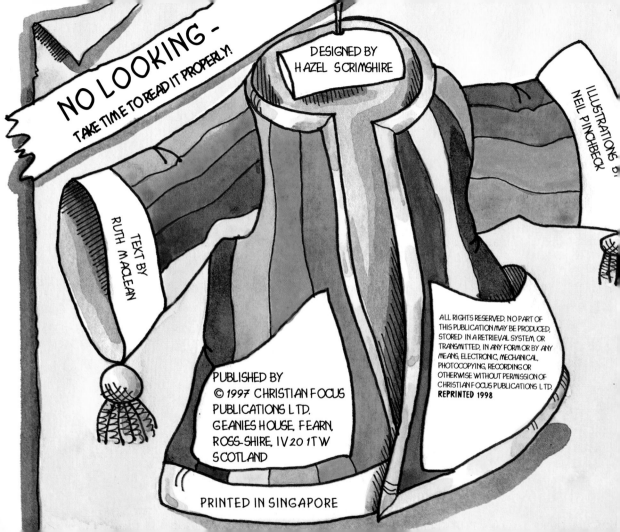

NO LOOKING -
TAKE TIME TO READ IT PROPERLY!

DESIGNED BY
HAZEL SCRIMSHIRE

ILLUSTRATIONS BY
NEIL PINCHBECK

TEXT BY
RUTH MACLEAN

PUBLISHED BY
© 1997 CHRISTIAN FOCUS
PUBLICATIONS LTD.
GEANIES HOUSE, FEARN,
ROSS-SHIRE, IV20 1TW
SCOTLAND

PRINTED IN SINGAPORE

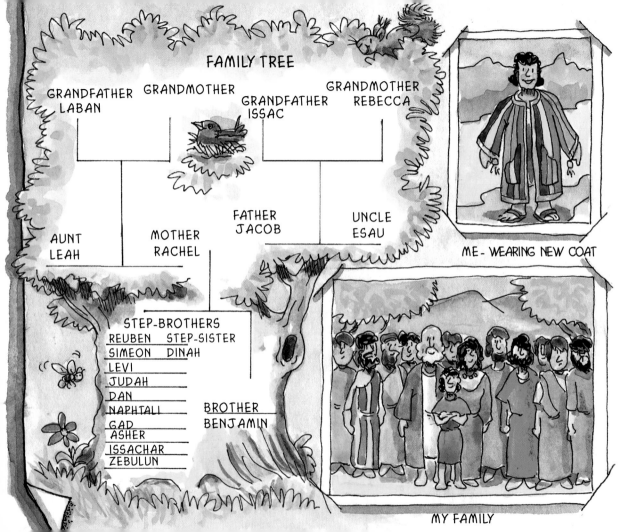

FAMILY TREE

GRANDFATHER LABAN
GRANDMOTHER
GRANDFATHER ISSAC
GRANDMOTHER REBECCA

FATHER JACOB
UNCLE ESAU

AUNT LEAH
MOTHER RACHEL

ME - WEARING NEW COAT

STEP-BROTHERS
REUBEN   STEP-SISTER
SIMEON   DINAH
LEVI
JUDAH
DAN
NAPHTALI
GAD
ASHER
ISSACHAR
ZEBULUN

BROTHER BENJAMIN

MY FAMILY

MY FAMILY

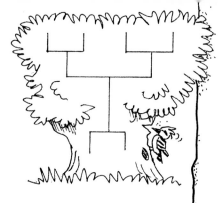

There were fourteen people in my family, including me! My dad's name was Jacob and my mum was called Rachel. I had eleven brothers - all of them were older than me, apart from one. We lived in a place called Canaan.

I was treated differently from the rest of my brothers. My father was quite old when I was born and he made a special fuss of me. My brothers

weren't too pleased about this and didn't like me very much. We were shepherds and our job was to look after the sheep. It didn't help things that when they did something wrong it was me who told Mum and Dad.

I remember when I was about seventeen years old, my dad gave me a special coat. It had long sleeves and was really smart! I loved that coat and was so proud of it. This just made my brothers jealous - they wouldn't even speak to me if they could help it. This was only the start of the trouble, worse was to come...

BAD DREAMS?

I've always been quite a dreamer. Some of the dreams I had were incredible! My brothers weren't too impressed when I told them my dreams. I suppose I can't really blame them. I remember one dream in particular, it was about sheaves of corn in the fields...

All of us were out in the fields working, we were tying up bundles of wheat. I saw that the bundle which I was working with, stood up really tall and straight. The bundles my brothers were working on came round to mine and began to bow down to my one.

My brothers took this dream to mean that I was going to rule over them. This made them dislike me *even more*! My dad was also annoyed when he heard the news. Maybe I should have kept quiet - the dreams upset them too much.

DREAM ON...

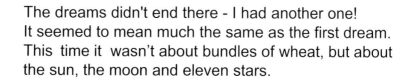

The dreams didn't end there - I had another one!
It seemed to mean much the same as the first dream.
This time it wasn't about bundles of wheat, but about
the sun, the moon and eleven stars.

*In the dream there were eleven stars, the
same number as I have brothers, the sun
and the moon. The sun, the moon and the
stars all bowed down to me.*

I told my father about this dream and *even he* ridiculed me about it.
He asked if I really thought that all the family would all bow down
to me? However, he did seriously think about what all these things
could possibly mean.

TRIP TO SHECHEM

I didn't realise how much my brothers hated me until my dad sent me to Shechem. My brothers were there, looking after the sheep. Father wanted me to go and find them and check that they were alright.

So I set off on the journey, but on arriving in Shechem they were nowhere to be seen. I searched everywhere! A man saw me and asked me who I was looking for. When I explained to him, he told me that they had moved on to a place called Dothan. So, on I travelled until at last I spotted them in the distance. Soon I'd find out how they were and be able to report back to my father.

My brothers had seen me coming too. I found out later that that was when they began to plot to get rid of me. In fact, they planned to *kill* me...!

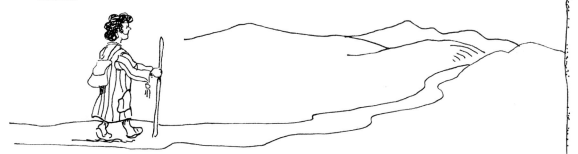

WELL, WELL, WELL!

'The dreamer is coming,' I heard them say, (that was what they called me). When I arrived at the place where they had stopped, they grabbed me, pulled off my special coat and threw me into a well! Fortunately the well was empty so I didn't get wet, but it wasn't very pleasant being stuck there! Meanwhile, they tucked into a meal and discussed what they were going to do with me.

After a while, I could hear the sound of strange voices. My brothers then lifted me out of the well. Standing around now were some camels and men, strangers to me. They were Ishmaelites. I heard my brother Judah suggest to the rest that nothing would be gained if they killed me, it would be just as well to sell me. I saw my brothers receive some money from the Ishmaelites and then I was handed over.

Later, I discovered that Reuben had been really sad and upset by what had happened - he wasn't there when I'd been sold. I wonder what he would have done to stop them?

MEANWHILE, BACK IN CANAAN...

It was years later before I discovered what my brothers had told my dad.

They had taken my precious coat, and ruined it! When my father saw it, covered in blood, he thought that a savage animal had eaten me. My brothers didn't tell him that they had killed a goat and dipped my coat in its blood, to trick him.

My father was sad for a very long time. He wept and tore his clothes, as people did when they were upset. Everyone tried to comfort him, but it was no use. He said he'd be sad about me until the day he died. I had been very special to him.

LIFE IN EGYPT

My new owners took me to Egypt, where I was
sold again, this time to an important man called
Potiphar. He was an officer of the king of Egypt.

As I look back, I can see that God was with me in
all these things. Potiphar seemed to see that too.
He gave me good jobs and put me in charge of his house. I was his
personal helper. I also learned to speak a new language. Everything
went so well while I was there and eventually I was put in charge of
all Potiphar's goods. The Lord blessed Potiphar and his household at
this time.

Sadly, Potiphar's wife told lies about me to her husband. He believed
her and was very angry with me. He had me arrested and then put
into prison. However, the Lord was with me while I was there, and I
discovered that God can work in _any_ situation.

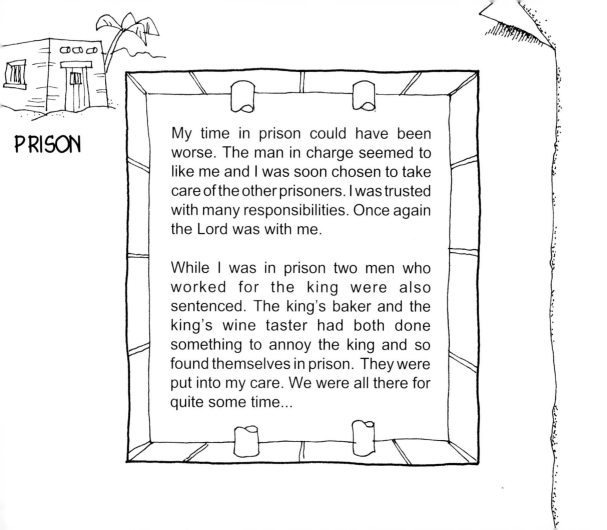

PRISON

My time in prison could have been worse. The man in charge seemed to like me and I was soon chosen to take care of the other prisoners. I was trusted with many responsibilities. Once again the Lord was with me.

While I was in prison two men who worked for the king were also sentenced. The king's baker and the king's wine taster had both done something to annoy the king and so found themselves in prison. They were put into my care. We were all there for quite some time...

STRANGE DREAMS

One morning, something very interesting happened. I discovered the kings' two servants were unhappy and worried. It turned out that they'd both had very strange dreams! They didn't know what they meant and wanted someone to explain them. I told them that it was only God who could give meaning to dreams. Then I asked them to tell me their dreams. The wine taster started first.

'I saw a vine with three branches. It began to bud, blossom and the grapes ripened. The king's cup was in my hand. I took the grapes from the vine and squeezed the juice into the cup. I gave the cup with the juice to the king.'

I explained that the branches stood for three days. Before three days passed the king would free him from prison and allow him to return to his job. I asked him to remember me when he was free again and tell the king about me. Perhaps I'd be able to get out of prison.

BAD NEWS FOR THE BAKER...

When the baker heard what the wine taster's dream was about, he was happy to talk of his dream.

'I saw myself with three baskets of bread on my head. In the top basket there was lots of baked food for the king. But birds were eating the food from the top basket.'

I was able to tell him what his dream meant too. The three baskets stood for three days. This dream however had a sad meaning. In three days the king would order his head to be cut off, then his body would be put out to hang on a pole for the birds to eat. Three days later, just as the dreams had shown, these things happened. The king had arranged a special birthday meal. During the feast he allowed the two men to be released from prison. The wine taster went back to his old job and served the wine there and then. Sadly the baker was killed.

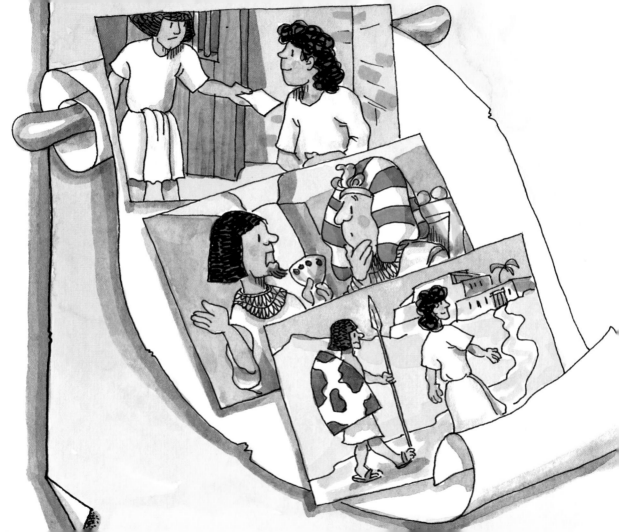

FREEDOM - AT LAST!

It was *two* years before anyone remembered about me! Then one day, I received a hurried message from the king which said that he wanted to see me, urgently!

Apparently the king had also been having strange dreams and was troubled by them. He had sent for all the wise men in the land of Egypt but no-one was able to tell him what his dreams meant. Somehow the wine server remembered me. He told the king what had happened in the prison and how he had promised to tell the king about me, but he had forgotten.

The guards led me out of prison and took me to the palace. I made sure that I was clean and smart and got ready to meet the king.

THE KING'S DREAMS — PART 1

The king told me that he'd had two dreams but no-one could explain them to him. He had been told that I would be able to help him. I explained that it was God who gave the ability to understand dreams. This is what the king told me.

'I was standing on the banks of the River Nile when up out of the river came seven cows, which looked fat and healthy. These cows ate the grass. Then there appeared seven more cows coming up out of the river, these cows looked dreadful, they were thin and didn't look good at all. Amazingly these cows ate up the fat ones. In spite of that, the thin cows still looked really skinny.'

He told me that he had woken up at that point, but then had *another* dream...

PART 2

The king then told me the other dream:

> *'This time my dream was about heads of grain. There was a stalk and on it there were growing seven good full heads, then seven thin heads grew. This time the thin heads ate the full heads up.'*

What does it all mean? he asked. I was able to tell him that the two dreams really meant the same thing - God was showing the king what was going to happen soon.

The number stood for seven years. The good things stood for seven good years, while the bad things stood for seven poor years. I told him, there would be seven years of plenty and then seven years of famine. Then I suggested a plan and waited to see what he would say.

NEW JOB

I had made the suggestion to Pharaoh, that he should find an able, wise and responsible man who could be put in charge of the food in the land. Someone sensible, who would make plans to store food in the good years and have it to use in the years of famine.

The king and his important people thought that my idea was a good one and they began to discuss who would be best for the job. Then Pharaoh asked me if *I* would do the job. He recognised that it was God who had told me what was going to happen - it was clear that God was with me. I was to be in charge of the land and everyone was to obey me.

I was only thirty years old and yet I was in a very responsible job. The king made sure I had everything that I needed. I was given fine clothes, a chariot, the king's own ring and a wife called Asenath. What a change from life in prison!

A SURPRISING VISIT

Throughout the first seven good years, I travelled around and made sure all the grain was collected in. We had so much we couldn't count it all! During this time I also became a father - my wife gave birth to two sons, Manasseh and Ephraim.

Things started to get difficult when the seven years of famine began. Other countries were also affected, but only Egypt had food in its stores. We opened the stores and sold the grain - people came from *all over* to buy grain from us.

One day, *a* group of men arrived to buy food - I could hardly believe my eyes - it was my brothers! They didn't recognise me and although I knew them right away, I pretended not to know them. They bowed down to me and this made me think of the dream I'd had many years before. They told me they had come from Canaan - my homeland! I accused them of being spies who just wanted to see what our land was like and where our defences were weak. They tried to convince me that this was not true - all they wanted to do was to buy grain! I decided to test their honesty...

THE BIG TEST!

The men from Canaan told me that they had a younger brother. To prove that they were telling the truth, I said that they would have to bring him to Egypt. Meanwhile, I put them in prison.

Three days later, I went and told them that if they really were honest men then everything would all be alright. I asked for one of them to stay in prison while the rest returned home. They were to bring their young brother back with them.

All the time I was with them, I had a man telling them what I was saying. I didn't let them know that I could speak their language. They didn't realize that I understood all that they said. I became upset when I heard them saying that they thought they were being punished for the way they had treated their brother Joseph years before. I managed to pull myself together and had Simeon tied up, he was the one that would have to stay.

Secretly, I arranged for their sacks to be filled with grain and for their money to be put back in their sacks. I gave them food for their journey too and sent them on their way home.

WHAT'S GOING ON?

Some time later, my brothers returned to Egypt. I was delighted when I saw that Benjamin was with them. I gave orders for them to be taken to my house and a feast was prepared for them.

Unfortunately, my brothers were suspicious of my actions. They were afraid and thought I wanted to attack them, (so one of my chief servants told me later). My brothers had poured out the whole story of how they had found their money in their sacks. They explained that they had returned this money and brought more back with them so that they could buy food. My servant told them not to worry, their grain *had* been paid for. He released Simeon and gave them what they needed to refresh themselves after their journey.

When I came home, they gave me gifts and bowed before me. I was glad to hear that our father was well and I was very moved to see Benjamin. In fact, it touched me so deeply that I had to leave the room! Once I had controlled my feelings we were able to have our meal. I made sure that Benjamin had a far greater share than anyone else. They still had no idea who I really was!

IT WASN'T ME!

Eventually it was time for my brothers to return home. Once again I secretly instructed my servants to fill all the sacks with food *and* the money. This time, I also told them to put my silver cup into the sack belonging to the youngest brother.

Soon after they had left, I sent my servant after them. They were shocked when he demanded to know why they had stolen his master's silver cup? My brothers denied this, but when they were searched, there was the cup for all to see - in Benjamin's sack!

They returned to my house where I was waiting for them. After apologising and trying to prove their innocence, they even offered to become my slaves! However I told them that only the one who was found to have my cup was to be my slave - the rest could go free.

At this, Judah came to me and reminded me of all that had happened to them since they had first set out to buy food. He also told me that he could not return without Benjamin as it would kill his aged father. He offered to stay, instead of Benjamin. I could stand the agony no longer.

THE SECRET'S OUT!

The servants were instructed to leave me so I could be alone with my brothers. Tears fell from my eyes as I told them that I was the one they had sold! 'Don't blame yourselves for what happened,' I said. 'God arranged it all for a purpose.'

I urged them to go home and tell my father everything and invite him to come and live in Egypt. Then they would have no need to worry about food during the famine. It was a great time of rejoicing for all of us, and we hugged each other and cried.

When Pharaoh heard of it, he and all his household were pleased too. He offered my brothers gifts and carts to bring their families back to Egypt.

Once they were ready, I sent them on their way and reminded them not to argue on the journey!

EGYPT

When Father was told the news he didn't believe it at first. But when he saw all the things which I had sent, he realised it must be true. He wanted to come and see me before he died, so they packed up and set off for Egypt.

While they were travelling, Jacob sent Judah ahead of the others to get exact directions where they should go. I went out to meet them in my chariot. I was *so happy* to see my father again. I gave him a big hug and started to cry.

I introduced my father to Pharaoh, and he blessed the king. Pharaoh wanted them to settle in the best part of the land - Goshen. I made sure they all had plenty of food, as the famine was so severe.

In fact the food shortage was so bad, that many people soon had no money left, so I exchanged food for their animals. Things got so difficult that eventually I bought their land from them too. When their next crop grew, they now had to give one-fifth of it to Pharaoh, the rest they could keep for themselves.

IT'S A PROMISE!

Father settled down in Goshen with the rest of the family, and lived there happily for seventeen years.

One day Father sent for me. He wanted me to promise him that he would not be buried in Egypt, but in Canaan, where his relatives were buried. Not long after I'd made this promise, news was brought to me that my dad was ill. I took my two sons and set off to see him. Although he was sick, he made a special effort to speak to me. He wanted to bless my sons and asked me to bring them close to him. I really thought that he was getting confused as he was determined to bless the younger one first. However, he assured me that this was the way it was meant to be.

My father also wanted to speak to the rest of my brothers. We gathered together for the last time, and Father gave us his blessing. When he died, I was *so* upset. We all mourned him for many days before setting off for Canaan. There we buried him in a cave which had been prepared for him. We were all very sad as we made our way back to Egypt.

GOD'S PLAN

After my father died, my brothers sent a message which made me very sad. They said that our father had left instructions, asking me to forgive them for all they had done. When they came to me and offered themselves as my slaves, I told them not to be afraid. They may have intended to harm me, but God had it all worked out. It was all part of his plan. I promised them kindly that I would provide for them and their children.

I stayed in Egypt for the rest of my days and was able to see my children's children and their children too! When I knew I would soon die, I called for my brothers and reminded them that God would look after them. He would take them to the land he had promised. I asked them to take my bones from Egypt when the time came, to go to the Promised Land, and bury them there.

When I think about all that happened to me and my family, I can see that God was watching over us - it's amazing what he can do if we let him have control!

WE READ ABOUT JOSEPH'S FAMILY AND LOOKED AT THEIR FAMILY TREE. CAN YOU FILL IN YOUR FAMILY DETAILS HERE?

Why not write something about your family?
Have any exciting things happened which you want to thank God for?